STEP Ladder

(300-word Level)

イソップ物語

Aesop's Fables

Aesop

イソップ

はじめに

みなさんは英語で何ができるようになりたいですか。

外国人と自由にコミュニケーションしたい
インターネット上の英語のサイトや、ペーパーバック、英字新聞を辞書なしで読めるようになりたい
字幕なしで洋画を見たい
受験や就職で有利になりたい
海外で活躍したい……

英語の基礎的な力、とりわけ読解力をつけるのに大切なのは、楽しみながら多読することです。数多くの英文に触れることによって、英語の発想や表現になじみ、英語の力が自然に身についてきます。

そうは言っても、何から手をつけていいのかわからないということはないでしょうか。やさしそうだと思って、外国の絵本や子ども向けの洋書を買ってはみたものの、知らない単語や表現ばかりが出てきて、途中で読むのをあきらめた経験がある方もいらっしゃるのではありませんか。

おすすめしたいのは、学習者向けにやさしく書かれた本から始めて、自分のレベルに合わせて、少しずつ難しいものに移っていく読み方です。

本書《ステップラダー・シリーズ》は、使用する単語を限定した、やさしい英語で書かれている英文リーダーで、初心者レベルの方でも、無理なく最後まで読めるように工夫されています。

みなさんが、楽しみながら英語の力をステップアップできるようになっています。

特長と使い方

●特長●

ステップラダー・シリーズは、世界の古典や名作などを、使用する単語を限定して、やさしい表現に書き改めた、英語初級～初中級者向けの英文リーダーです。見開きごとのあらすじや、すべての単語の意味が載ったワードリストなど、初心者レベルでも負担なく、英文が読めるように構成されています。無料音声ダウンロード付きですので、文字と音声の両面で読書を楽しむことができます。

ステップ	使用語彙数	対象レベル	英検	CEFR
STEP 1	300語	中学1年生程度	5級	A1
STEP 2	600語	中学2年生程度	4級	A1
STEP 3	900語	中学3年生程度	3級	A2

●使い方●

- 本文以外のパートはすべてヘルプです。できるだけ本文に集中して読みましょう。
- 日本語の語順に訳して読むと速く読むことができません。文の頭から順番に、意味のかたまりごとに理解するようにしましょう。
- すべてを100パーセント理解しようとせず、ところどころ想像で補うようにして、ストーリーに集中する方が、楽に楽しく読めます。
- 黙読する、音読する、音声に合わせて読む、音声だけを聞くなど、いろいろな読み方をしてみましょう。

●無料音声ダウンロード●

本書の朗読音声(MP3形式)を、下記URLとQRコードから無料でダウンロードすることができます。

www.ibcpub.co.jp/step_ladder/0642/

※PCや端末、ソフトウェアの操作・再生方法については、編集部ではお答えできません。製造元にお問い合わせいただくか、インターネットで検索するなどして解決してください。

●構成●

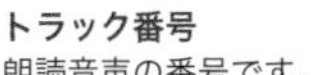

語数表示
開いたページの単語数と、読んできた総単語数が確認できます。

2

01 [1]A hare lived high on a mountain near a river.

His neighbor was a tortoise.

The hare had long legs.
He could run faster than many animals.

The tortoise had a big shell
and short little legs.

Every day he walked slowly to the river
on his flat feet.

He swam in the river,
ate some grass,
and slowly walked home.

うさぎの隣人はカメでした。うさぎは足が速く、カメはゆっくり歩きます。ある日、カメはうさぎが自分を見つめていることに気がつきました。

The Hare and the Tortoise 3

[2]One day,
the tortoise found the hare staring at him.

The hare was smiling.

(75[75] words)

◆KEYWORDS

□hare [héəʳ]
□tortoise [tɔ́ːʳtəs]
□mountain [máuntən]
□river [rívəʳ]
□neighbor [néibəʳ]
□was [wɑ́ːz] < is
□could [kúd] < can
□than [ðən]
□shell [ʃél]
□slowly [slóuli]
□flat [flǽt]
□ate [éit] < eat
□grass [grǽs]
□*one day*
□stare [stéəʳ]
□smile [smáil]

◆KEY SENTENCES (☞ p. 64)

[1] A hare lived / high on a mountain / near a river.
[2] One day, / the tortoise found the hare / staring at him.

あらすじ
本文のおおまかな内容がわかります。

キーワード
使用語彙以外で使われている初出の単語、熟語のリストです。発音記号の読み方は次ページの表を参考にしてください。

キーセンテンス
長い文や難しい表現の文を、意味単位に区切って紹介しています。表示のページに訳があります。

キーワードについて

1. 語尾が規則変化する単語は原形、不規則変化語は本文で出てきた形を見出しにしています。

   例 studies/studying/studied → study
   goes/going → go
   went → went
   gone → gone

2. 熟語に含まれる所有格の人称代名詞(my, your, his/her, theirなど)は one's に、再帰代名詞(myself, yourselfなど)は oneself に置き換えています。

   例 do your best → do one's best
   enjoy myself → enjoy oneself

3. 熟語に含まれるbe動詞 (is, are, was, were)は原形のbeに置き換えています。

   例 was going to → be going to

発音記号表 

●母音●

/ɑ/	hot, lot
/ɑː/	arm, art, car, hard, march, park, father
/æ/	ask, bag, cat, dance, hand, man, thank
/aɪ/	ice, nice, rice, time, white, buy, eye, fly
/aɪə^r/	fire, tire
/aʊ/	brown, down, now, house, mouth, out
/aʊə^r/	flower, shower, tower, hour
/e/	bed, egg, friend, head, help, letter, pet, red
/eɪ/	cake, make, face, game, name, day, play
/eə^r/	care, chair, hair
/ɪ/	big, fish, give, listen, milk, pink, sing
/iː/	eat, read, speak, green, meet, week, people
/ɪə^r/	dear, ear, near, year
/oʊ/	cold, go, home, note, old, coat, know
/ɔː/	all, ball, call, talk, walk
/ɔː^r/	door, more, short
/ɔɪ/	boy, enjoy, toy
/ʊ/	book, cook, foot, good, look, put
/uː/	food, room, school, fruit, juice
/ʊə^r/	pure, sure
/əː^r/	bird, girl, third, learn, turn, work
/ʌ/	bus, club, jump, lunch, run, love, mother
/ə/	about, o'clock
/i/	easy, money, very

●子音●

/b/	bag, ball, bed, big, book, club, job
/d/	desk, dog, door, cold, food, friend
/f/	face, finger, fish, food, half, if, laugh
/g/	game, girl, go, good, big, dog, egg
/h/	hair, hand, happy, home, hot
/j/	yellow, yes, young
/k/	cake, cook, king, desk, look, milk, pink, talk
/l/	learn, leg, little, look, animal, girl, school
/m/	make, mother, movie, home, name, room, time
/n/	know, name, night, noon, pen, run, train
/p/	park, pencil, pet, pink, cap, help, jump, stop
/r/	read, red, rice, room, run, write
/s/	say, see, song, study, summer, bus, face, ice
/t/	talk, teacher, time, train, cat, foot, hat, night
/v/	very, video, visit, five, give, have, love, movie
/w/	walk, want, week, woman, work
/z/	zero, zoo, clothes, has, music, nose
/ʃ/	ship, short, English, fish, station
/ʒ/	measure, leisure, television
/ŋ/	king, long, sing, spring, English, drink, thank
/tʃ/	chair, cheap, catch, lunch, march, teacher, watch
/θ/	thank, think, thursday, birthday, month, mouth, tooth
/ð/	they, this, then, bathe, brother, father, mother
/dʒ/	Japan, jump, junior, bridge, change, enjoy, orange

Contents

『イソップ物語』について

『イソップ物語』は世界中の誰もが知る、世代を超えて愛されてきた寓話の作品集です。作者のイソップ(アイソーポス)は、紀元前5世紀ごろの古代ギリシャに実在したとされる奴隷です。寓話を作り、語るのが上手であったと、ヘロドトスの『歴史』にその名が記されています。

「寓話」とは動物を主人公にした物語のことです。イソップは小アジアの出身で、そこに伝わる民話などを基にしていると言われていますが、すべての逸話が彼自身によって作られたわけではありません。それ以降の時代にも、小アジアやアフリカの民間伝承などが集められ、追加・訂正されながら現存する形になったと考えられています。この寓話集は、国から国へ、人から人へ、親から子へ、と語り継がれるなかで、人生における教訓や道徳観念を、子どもや文字の読めない人にも分かりやすく伝えるのに、大いに役立ってきました。

日本には1593年、イエズス会の宣教師がラテン語から翻訳して紹介したとされています。江戸時代に『伊曽保物語』として出版され、明治時代には英語からの翻訳が進み、小学校の教科書にも採用されたことから、広く親しまれるようになりました。本書に掲載されている「ウサギとカメ」などはすっかり日本の昔話として定着し、語り継がれています。元々は日本の昔話ではない、と知ったら驚く方も多いことでしょう。

イソップ物語が庶民的で親しみやすいのは、どこか滑稽で人間臭い登場動物&人物たちに、私たち自身の姿が投影されていると感じるからでしょう。地域・文化・言語に関係なく、人間は皆同じようなことで悩み、失敗し、笑い、を繰り返してきたのだと感じさせてくれる。これこそが、今なお世界中の人々から愛され続けている理由なのではないでしょうか。

The Hare and the Tortoise

[1] A hare lived high on a mountain near a river.

His neighbor was a tortoise.

The hare had long legs.
He could run faster than many animals.

The tortoise had a big shell
and short little legs.

Every day he walked slowly to the river
on his flat feet.

He swam in the river,
ate some grass,
and slowly walked home.

ウサギの隣人はカメでした。ウサギは足が速く、カメはゆっくり歩きます。
ある日、カメはウサギが自分を見つめていることに気がつきました。

2 One day,
the tortoise found the hare staring at him.

The hare was smiling.

(75[75] words)

◆KEYWORDS

- ☐ **hare** [héə^r]
- ☐ **tortoise** [tɔ́ː^{r}təs]
- ☐ **mountain** [máʊntən]
- ☐ **river** [rívə^r]
- ☐ **neighbor** [néɪbə^r]
- ☐ **was** [wɑːz] < is
- ☐ **could** [kʊ́d] < can
- ☐ **than** [ðən]
- ☐ **shell** [ʃél]
- ☐ **slowly** [slóʊli]
- ☐ **flat** [flǽt]
- ☐ **ate** [éɪt] < eat
- ☐ **grass** [grǽs]
- ☐ *one day*
- ☐ **stare** [stéə^r]
- ☐ **smile** [smáɪl]

◆KEY SENTENCES (☞ p. 64)

1 A hare lived / high on a mountain / near a river.

2 One day, / the tortoise found the hare / staring at him.

It looked like he was laughing.

“Why are you laughing?”
the tortoise asked.

“Because you are so funny,”
the hare said.
“You have no legs!”

3 The tortoise tried to show the hare
that he had legs.

But his shell hid them,
so the hare kept laughing.

4 The tortoise did not like the hare
laughing at him.

(56[131] words)

ウサギはカメに「君はとても面白いな。足がない」と言って笑いました。カメは足を見せようとしましたが、足は甲らに隠れて見えませんでした。

◆ KEYWORDS

☐ **laugh** [lǽf]
☐ **why** [hwáɪ]
☐ **funny** [fʌ́ni]
☐ **said** [séd] < say
☐ **try** [tráɪ]
☐ **show** [ʃóʊ]
☐ **hid** [híd] < hide
☐ **kept** [képt] < keep

◆ KEY SENTENCES (☞ p. 64)

3 The tortoise tried to show the hare / that / he had legs.

4 The tortoise did not like the hare / laughing at him.

"Race me!"
said the tortoise.
"Then you will see that I have legs."

"Race? You?"
said the hare.
"To where?"

"[5]Mr. Fox over there can be our judge.
He will decide the course
and the finish line.
Do you agree?"

[6]The hare laughed even harder,
thinking the tortoise was crazy.

"Sure!" he said.

「競争しよう！」とカメは言い、「そこにいるキツネが審判だ。コースとゴールを決めてもらっていいか」と聞くと、ウサギは大笑いで同意しました。

The tortoise and the hare visited Mr. Fox to tell him the tortoise's idea.

(67[198] words)

◆ KEYWORDS

- ☐ **race** [réɪs]
- ☐ **fox** [fɑ́:ks]
- ☐ *over there*
- ☐ **judge** [dʒʌ́dʒ]
- ☐ **decide** [dɪ̀sáɪd]
- ☐ **finish** [fínɪʃ]
- ☐ **line** [láɪn]
- ☐ *finish line*
- ☐ **agree** [əgrí:]
- ☐ **even** [í:vɪn]
- ☐ **crazy** [kréɪzi]
- ☐ **tell** [tél]

◆ KEY SENTENCES (☞ p. 64)

5 Mr. Fox / over there / can be our judge.

6 The hare laughed / even harder, / thinking / the tortoise was crazy.

They asked Mr. Fox to watch their race.

The fox agreed
and made a good course for them.

7 The course went down the mountain,
around the river,
and through the woods to a city
many miles away.

キツネは、山を下って川を回り、森を抜けて町までのコースを作りました。
ウサギはすぐに山を駆け下り、カメもゆっくりと山を下り始めました。

"Well,
goodbye,"
said the hare to the tortoise.

"I'll see you again in a day or two!"

Then the hare disappeared,
running down the mountain.

The tortoise started to walk slowly
down the mountain too.

(72[270] words)

◆ KEYWORDS

- ☐ **made** [méɪd] < make
- ☐ *go down*
- ☐ **through** [θrúː]
- ☐ **wood** [wʊ́d]
- ☐ **city** [síti]
- ☐ **mile** [máɪl]
- ☐ **away** [əwéɪ]
- ☐ **again** [əgén]
- ☐ *in a day or two*
- ☐ **disappear** [dìsəpíə^{r}]

◆ KEY SENTENCES (☞ p. 64)

7 The course went down the mountain, / around the river, / and through the woods / to a city / many miles away.

The hare ran for one or two miles.

Then he felt tired,
so he looked for a place to rest.
He found a nice tree and lay down under it.

He looked down the road.
He did not see the tortoise.

The tortoise was still very far behind
on the course.

8 "That tortoise will not catch up with me,"
thought the hare.
9 "I will sleep here for a little while
and then run again in the evening."

Soon, he was asleep.

(81[351] words)

しばらく走って疲れたウサギは、道を見下ろしてもカメの姿が見えないので、
夕方になったらまた走ろうと、木の下で横になり寝てしまいました。

◆KEYWORDS

□ **ran** [rǽn] < run
□ **felt** [félt] < feel
□ **tired** [táɪə^{r}d]
□ *look for*
□ **place** [pléɪs]
□ **rest** [rést]
□ **found** [fáʊnd] < find
□ **tree** [tríː]
□ **lay** [léɪ] < lie
□ *lie down*
□ **road** [róʊd]
□ **still** [stíl]
□ **far** [fɑ́ː^{r}]
□ *far behind*
□ *catch up with*
□ **thought** [θɔ́ːt] < think
□ **sleep** [slíːp]
□ **while** [^{h}wáɪl]
□ *for a while*
□ **asleep** [əslíːp]

◆KEY SENTENCES (☞ p. 64)

8 "That tortoise / will not / catch up with me," / thought the hare.

9 "I will sleep here / for a little while / and then / run again / in the evening."

Meanwhile,
the tortoise walked slowly
down the mountain.
It took him all afternoon.

Then he walked slowly around the river.
It took him all night.

In the morning,
he walked through the woods.

Slowly but surely,
slowly but surely,
he walked along the course.

He never stopped.

カメはゆっくり、確実にコースに沿って歩き、決して立ち止まりませんでした。そして一日中、ひと晩中歩いた後、ついに町に近づきました。

11 And,
after walking all day and all night,
he was finally close to the city.

(62[413] words)

◆KEYWORDS

- ☐ **meanwhile** [mí:nwàɪl]
- ☐ **took** [tʊ́k] < take
- ☐ **surely** [ʃʊ́əʳli]
- ☐ **along** [əlɔ́:ŋ]
- ☐ **never** [névəʳ]
- ☐ **finally** [fáɪnəli]
- ☐ **close to**

◆KEY SENTENCES (☞ p. 64)

10 It took him / all afternoon.

11 And, / after walking / all day and all night, / he was finally / close to the city.

In the morning,
the hare woke up.

12 When he saw the morning sun shining,
he jumped to his feet.

“Oh, no!
I was asleep all night!”
cried the hare.

He ran down the mountain.
Then he quickly crossed the river.
Then he ran through the woods.

He ran very fast.
13 But when he reached the city,
what do you think he saw there?

ウサギは朝日が輝いているのを見て飛び起きると、とても速く走りました。
しかし町に着いたとき、ウサギはカメが休んでいるのが見えました。

He saw the tortoise resting.
Mr. Fox was by his side.

(74 [487] words)

◆KEYWORDS

- ☐ **woke** [wóʊk] < wake
- ☐ *wake up*
- ☐ **shine** [ʃáɪn]
- ☐ *jump to one's feet*
- ☐ **cry** [kráɪ]
- ☐ **quickly** [kwíkli]
- ☐ **cross** [krɔ́ːs]
- ☐ *run through*
- ☐ **reach** [ríːtʃ]
- ☐ **side** [sáɪd]
- ☐ *by one's side*

◆KEY SENTENCES (☞ p. 64)

12 When he saw the morning sun / shining, / he jumped to his feet.

13 But / when he reached the city, / what do you think / he saw / there?

"The tortoise won the race!"
said Mr. Fox.

14 "He may be slow,
but he works hard and never stops to rest."

The hare shook his head.
He could not believe he lost the race.

"Next time,
don't be so arrogant!"
said Mr. Fox.

15 "Working slowly but surely
will win the race."

(51 [538] words)

キツネは「レースはカメの勝ち」と言い、それから、「ゆっくりと、しかし確実に働くことが、勝利につながるのさ」と言いました。

◆KEYWORDS

- ☐ **won** [wʌ́n] < win
- ☐ **slow** [slóʊ]
- ☐ **shook** [ʃʊ́k] < shake
- ☐ *shake one's head*
- ☐ **believe** [bɪlíːv]
- ☐ **lost** [lɔ́ːst] < lose
- ☐ **arrogant** [érəgənt]
- ☐ **win** [wín]

◆KEY SENTENCES (☞ p. 65)

14 "He may be slow, / but / he works hard / and / never stops / to rest."

15 "Working slowly / but surely / will win the race."

The Boy Who Cried Wolf

A long time ago,
many farmers lived near a forest.

16 And many animals lived in this forest,
including big wolves.

In the summer,
the farmers did not mind the wolves.

17 In the summer,
there were many animals in the forest
and the wolves had lots to eat.

So they left the farmers alone.

But in the winter,
the forest became cold.

森の近くに多くの農民が住み、森にはオオカミと多くの動物が住んでいました。冬になると獲物が見つけられずにオオカミはお腹をすかせました。

The wolves could not find animals to eat. They became very hungry.

(73[611] words)

◆KEYWORDS

- ☐ **wolf** [wʊ́lf]
- ☐ **ago** [əgóʊ]
- ☐ **farmer** [fɑ́:^{r}mə^{r}]
- ☐ **forest** [fɔ́:rəst]
- ☐ **including** [ìnklú:dɪŋ]
- ☐ **mind** [máɪnd]
- ☐ **were** [wə́:^{r}] < are
- ☐ **left** [léft] < leave
- ☐ **alone** [əlóʊn]
- ☐ *leave ~ alone*
- ☐ **became** [bɪkéɪm] < become

◆KEY SENTENCES (☞ p. 65)

[16] And / many animals lived / in this forest, / including big wolves.

[17] In the summer, / there were many animals / in the forest / and / the wolves had lots / to eat.

18 One day,
the wolves came out of the forest
to look for food.

19 They walked through the hills
where the farmers lived with their sheep.

These farmers are called shepherds.

The wolves found that
the sheep were easy to hunt.

They started to kill many sheep.
The shepherds became afraid of
the wolves.

The shepherds wanted to stop the wolves.
What could they do?

(64[675] words)

羊と暮らす農民は羊飼いと呼ばれます。食べ物を探して森から出てきたオオカミは羊を殺し始めました。羊飼いたちはオオカミを止めようとしました。

◆ KEYWORDS

- ☐ **hill** [híl]
- ☐ **sheep** [ʃíːp]
- ☐ **shepherd** [ʃépəʳd]
- ☐ **easy** [íːzi]
- ☐ **hunt** [hʌ́nt]
- ☐ **kill** [kíl]
- ☐ **afraid** [əfréɪd]

◆ KEY SENTENCES (☞ p. 65)

18 One day, / the wolves came out of the forest / to look for food.

19 They walked through the hills / where the farmers lived / with their sheep.

They had an idea to help one another.

Any time a shepherd saw a wolf,
he cried,
"Wolf! Wolf!"

Then all the other shepherds came
from all over the hills.

All together,
they would chase the wolf away.

The shepherds did this for several days.
They saw that it worked very well.

They were able to protect their sheep
and each other.

羊飼いはオオカミを見つけると「オオカミだ！」と叫びました。すると、他の羊飼いたちが集まり、協力してオオカミを追い払うことができました。

21 All they had to do was shout,
"Wolf! Wolf!"
and every shepherd came to help
at any time of day or night.

Working together,
they were able to chase the wolves away.

(94[769] words)

◆KEYWORDS

- □ **another** [ənʌ́ðəʳ]
- □ *one another*
- □ *any time*
- □ **together** [təgéðəʳ]
- □ **would** [wʊ́d] < will
- □ **chase** [tʃéɪs]
- □ *chase away*
- □ **several** [sévərəl]
- □ **able** [éɪbəl]
- □ **protect** [prətékt]
- □ **each** [íːtʃ]
- □ *each other*
- □ **shout** [ʃáʊt]
- □ *at any time of day or night*

◆KEY SENTENCES (☞ p. 65)

20 They saw / that / it worked very well.

21 All they had to do / was shout, / "Wolf! Wolf!" / and / every shepherd came to help / at any time of day or night.

Then,
one day,
one of the older shepherds had to
go to town for several days.

22 He told his son to watch the sheep
while he was gone.

But the son was a coward.

He was afraid of many things.
And he was very afraid of wolves!

“Remember,
you are not alone,”
the old shepherd told his son.

ある日、年老いた羊飼いの一人が数日町に行かなければならず、息子に自分がいない間、羊を見張るように言いました。しかし息子は臆病者でした。

23 "If you see a wolf,
just shout 'Wolf! Wolf!'
and the other shepherds will come
to help you."

(76[845] words)

◆KEYWORDS

- ☐ **town** [táʊn]
- ☐ **told** [tóʊld] < tell
- ☐ **gone** [gɔ́ːn] < go
- ☐ **coward** [káʊəʳd]
- ☐ **thing** [θíŋ]
- ☐ **remember** [rɪmémbəʳ]
- ☐ **if** [ɪf]
- ☐ **will** [wíl]

◆KEY SENTENCES (☞ p. 65)

22 He told his son / to watch the sheep / while he was gone.

23 "If you see a wolf, / just shout / 'Wolf! Wolf!' / and / the other shepherds will come / to help you."

24 The boy asked his father not to go,
but the old shepherd had to leave.

25 So the boy sat next to his sheep,
holding his stick in fear.

The sun went down
and the moon came up.

Suddenly,
he heard a noise come
from behind the trees.
He jumped up in fear.

Was that a wolf?

The boy did not stop to think.
He was very afraid!

少年は羊の隣に座り、恐怖の中で杖を握っていました。月が出たころ、とつぜん木陰から物音が聞こえました。少年は「オオカミだ！」と叫びました。

He cried out,
"Wolf! Wolf!"

All through the hills,
the other shepherds heard the boy's cry.

(83 [928] words)

◆ KEYWORDS

- ☐ **stick** [stík]
- ☐ **fear** [fíə^{r}]
- ☐ *in fear*
- ☐ **moon** [mú:n]
- ☐ **suddenly** [sʌ́dənli]
- ☐ **heard** [hə́:^{r}d] < hear
- ☐ **noise** [nɔ́ɪz]
- ☐ *cry out*

◆ KEY SENTENCES (☞ p. 65)

24 The boy asked his father / not to go, / but / the old shepherd had to leave.

25 So / the boy sat next to his sheep, / holding his stick / in fear.

Young shepherds and old shepherds
all ran to the boy.
They waved their sticks
and picked up stones.

26 They gathered near the boy,
ready to fight the wolves.

But what do you think they saw?
Not a single wolf!
All they saw was a boy crying in fear.

27 "What is the matter?"
they asked the boy.
"There is no wolf here!"

The boy just shook in fear,
holding his stick.

(70[998] words)

羊飼いたちがみな棒や石を手に取り少年のもとに走ってきました。しかしオオカミは一匹もいません。彼らは恐怖で泣いている少年を見ただけでした。

◆ KEYWORDS

- ☐ **wave** [wéɪv]
- ☐ **pick** [pík]
- ☐ *pick up*
- ☐ **stone** [stóʊn]
- ☐ **gather** [gǽðəʳ]
- ☐ *ready to*
- ☐ **fight** [fáɪt]
- ☐ **single** [síŋgəl]
- ☐ **matter** [mǽtəʳ]

◆ KEY SENTENCES (☞ p. 66)

26 They gathered near the boy, / ready to fight the wolves.

27 "What is the matter?" / they asked the boy.

28 "You made us leave our warm beds!"
the shepherds said to the boy.

They shook their heads and went home.
The boy was alone with his sheep again.

The shepherds returned home.
When they were in bed,
they heard the boy calling for them again.

29 "Wolf! Wolf!"
came the boy's voice from across the hills.
"Wolf! Wolf!"

Again,
the shepherds jumped out of bed.

They ran across the hills to help the boy.

羊飼いたちが家に帰りベッドに入っていると、少年がまた呼んでいるのが聞こえました。彼らはベッドから飛び出し丘の向こうへ走っていきました。

They picked up sticks and stones.

But when they came to the boy,
what do you think they saw?

(92[1,090] words)

◆**KEYWORDS**

☐ **warm** [wɔ́ːʳm]
☐ **return** [rɪtə́ːʳn]
☐ *call for*
☐ **voice** [vɔ́ɪs]
☐ **across** [əkrɔ́ːs]

◆**KEY SENTENCES** (☞ p. 66)

28 "You made us leave / our warm beds!" / the shepherds said / to the boy.

29 "Wolf! Wolf!" / came the boy's voice / from across the hills.

Again, they found no wolves!

“There is no wolf here!”
they said to the boy.
[30]“You are just seeing shadows
made by the moon!”

The shepherds became very angry.
“We didn’t come here to fight shadows!”
they told the boy.

“I thought it was a wolf,”
said the boy,
still shaking in fear.

“[31]How can you think a shadow is a wolf?
You stupid boy.
A real wolf is nothing like the shadows.”

またもオオカミはいませんでした。少年は月の影をオオカミだと思ったのでした。羊飼いたちはとても怒り、寒くて眠い中を歩いて帰っていきました。

Then they all walked away,
cold and sleepy and still angry.

(84[1,174] words)

◆KEYWORDS

☐ **shadow** [ʃǽdòʊ]
☐ **angry** [ǽŋgri]
☐ **shake** [ʃéɪk]
☐ *How can you*
☐ **stupid** [stúːpɪd]
☐ **real** [ríːl]
☐ **nothing** [nʌ́θɪŋ]
☐ *nothing like*
☐ **sleepy** [slíːpi]

◆KEY SENTENCES (☞ p. 66)

30 "You are just seeing shadows / made by the moon!"
31 How can you think / a shadow is a wolf?

32 The shepherds were walking back home
when they heard the boy cry out
a third time.

"Wolf! Wolf!"
the boy called from across the hills.

But the shepherds shook their heads.

"No!"
they said.

"Not again.
That boy is seeing moon shadows.
We will not run back again
just for shadows!"

羊飼いたちが家に帰ろうとしたとき、少年が3回目の叫び声を上げるのが聞こえました。彼らは「またか」と言い、家に帰ると寝てしまいました。

33 Saying this,
they walked home.

They all went to bed
and didn't hear anything else that night.

(68[1,242] words)

◆ KEYWORDS

□ *Not again.*	□ **anything** [éniθìŋ]
□ **hear** [híəʳ]	□ **else** [éls]

◆ KEY SENTENCES (☞ p. 66)

32 The shepherds were walking back home / when they heard the boy / cry out / a third time.

33 Saying this, / they walked home.

34 But sadly,
this time it really was a wolf!

And many other wolves came!

The shepherd boy called for help,
but the wolves ate all the sheep.

Finally,
the wolves even ate
the foolish shepherd boy.

35 When the boy's father came home
several days later,
his son and his sheep were gone.

(52[1,294] words)

悲しいことに、今度は本当にオオカミでした。オオカミたちは羊をみな食べてしまい、最後には、羊飼いの少年まで食べてしまいました。

◆ KEYWORDS

- ☐ **sadly** [sǽdli]
- ☐ **really** [rí:li]
- ☐ *call for help*
- ☐ **foolish** [fú:lɪʃ]
- ☐ **later** [léɪtəʳ]

◆ KEY SENTENCES (☞ p. 66)

34 But sadly, / this time / it really was a wolf!

35 When the boy's father came home / several days later, / his son and his sheep were gone.

The old shepherd made a grave for his son.

What do you think he wrote on the marker?

36 "If you cry 'wolf' for shadows,
nobody will come to help
when a real wolf comes."

(34[1,328] words)

年老いた羊飼いが息子のために墓を作りました。彼は墓に「影をオオカミだと叫ぶと、本物のオオカミが来たときに誰も助けに来ない」と書きました。

◆ KEYWORDS

☐ **grave** [gréɪv]
☐ **wrote** [róʊt] < write
☐ **marker** [mɑ́ːʳkəʳ]
☐ **nobody** [nóʊbədi]

◆ KEY SENTENCES (☞ p. 66)

36 "If you cry 'wolf' for shadows, / nobody will come to help / when a real wolf comes."

The Committee of Mice

A long time ago,
there was an old mill near a small lake.

37 The mill had hundreds of mice
living in its walls.

The mice and their families lived there
for two or three hundred years.
They were very happy there.

Then,
one day,
a young miller came along.

He wanted to use the old mill.
38 So he walked around to look at it.

古い製粉所の壁の中に何百匹ものネズミが住んでいました。ある日若い製粉業者がやってきて見て回ったあと、ネコを連れて帰ってきました。

He soon found out
that the hundreds of mice lived there.

So the miller went away
and came back with a cat!

(86[1,414] words)

◆ **KEYWORDS**

- ☐ **committee** [kəmíti]
- ☐ **mice** [máɪs] < mouse
- ☐ **mill** [míl]
- ☐ **lake** [léɪk]
- ☐ **wall** [wɔ́:l]
- ☐ **miller** [mílə^{r}]
- ☐ *come along*
- ☐ *walk around*
- ☐ *find out*

◆ **KEY SENTENCES** (☞ p. 66)

37 The mill had hundreds of mice / living / in its walls.

38 So / he walked around / to look at it.

The cat sat on top of the grain.

39 All the mice took their children
and ran quickly up to the next floor.

The cat was asleep for most of the day.
Two or three times
she woke up to wash her face.

Then,
late at night,
she finally stood up.

She stretched out her body
and started to hunt.

She was a very good hunter.

ネコは一日のうちほとんどを穀物の上で寝ていましたが、夜遅くにやっと立ち上がり、狩りを始めると、太ったネズミを5、6匹捕まえて食べました。

[40]She caught and ate
five or six of the fattest mice.

(76[1,490] words)

◆KEYWORDS

- ☐ **top** [tɑ́:p]
- ☐ **grain** [gréɪn]
- ☐ **children** [tʃíldrən] < child
- ☐ **most** [móʊst]
- ☐ **wash** [wɑ́:ʃ]
- ☐ *late at night*
- ☐ **stood** [stʊ́d] < stand
- ☐ *stand up*
- ☐ **stretch** [strétʃ]
- ☐ *stretch out*
- ☐ **hunter** [hʌ́ntəʳ]
- ☐ **caught** [kɔ́:t] < catch
- ☐ **fat** [fǽt]

◆KEY SENTENCES (☞ p. 67)

[39]All the mice took their children / and / ran quickly up / to the next floor.

[40]She caught and ate / five or six / of the fattest mice.

The next night the same thing happened.
And the next,
and the next.

Even though the mice tried to hide,
the cat always caught five or six mice.

41 The biggest problem was that
the mice could not hear her.

She was so quiet.
42 The mice only saw her big,
green eyes when it was too late.

(56[1,546] words)

次の日も次の日も、ネコは5、6匹のネズミを捕まえました。ネズミたちには彼女の音が聞こえず、彼女の大きな目を見たときにはすでに手遅れでした。

◆ KEYWORDS

- ☐ **same** [séɪm]
- ☐ **happen** [hǽpən]
- ☐ **though** [ðóʊ]
- ☐ *even though*
- ☐ **hide** [háɪd]
- ☐ **always** [ɔ́ːlwèɪz]
- ☐ **problem** [prɑ́ːbləm]
- ☐ **quiet** [kwáɪət]
- ☐ **only** [óʊnli]

◆ KEY SENTENCES (☞ p. 67)

41 The biggest problem was / that / the mice could not hear her.

42 The mice only saw / her big, green eyes / when it was too late.

Soon,
every family in the mill lost
a brother or sister to the cat.

43 They asked the wisest mice in Mouse-town
to hold a committee meeting.

They needed to talk about the cat problem.

So,
one night,
all the wise mice held a meeting.
They started to talk.

44 They said they could run and hide
if they could hear the cat coming.
But how could they do that?

ネズミたちが会議を開くと、彼らはネコが来るのさえ聞こえれば逃げたり隠れたりできると言いました。1匹の利口な若いネズミが話し始めました。

One very smart young mouse stood up and started to speak.

(79[1,625] words)

◆KEYWORDS

☐ **wise** [wáɪz]
☐ **Mouse-town** [màʊstáʊn]
☐ *hold a meeting*
☐ **need** [níːd]
☐ **held** [héld] < hold
☐ **smart** [smɑ́ːʳt]
☐ **mouse** [máʊs]

◆KEY SENTENCES (☞ p. 67)

43 They asked the wisest mice / in Mouse-town / to hold a committee meeting.

44 They said / they could run and hide / if they could hear / the cat coming.

“I have an idea!”
he said.

“45 When men want to warn others
about danger,
they always send someone with a big bell.

46 Now,
if the cat wears a bell around her neck,
it will ring every time she moves.

Then we will all know that she is coming.

Let us tie a bell with some rope
around the neck of the cat!”

(62[1,687] words)

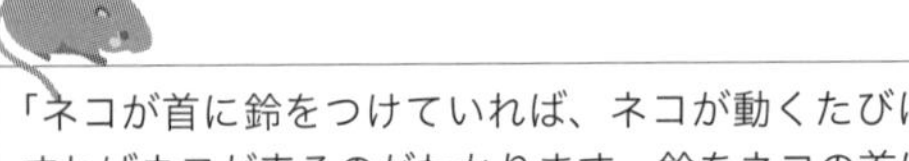

「ネコが首に鈴をつけていれば、ネコが動くたびに鈴が鳴るでしょう。そうすればネコが来るのがわかります。鈴をネコの首にひもで結びましょう！」

◆KEYWORDS

- ☐ **warn** [wɔ́ː^{r}n]
- ☐ **danger** [déɪndʒə^r]
- ☐ **send** [sénd]
- ☐ **wear** [wéə^r]
- ☐ **bell** [bél]
- ☐ **ring** [ríŋ]
- ☐ *every time*
- ☐ **let** [lét]
- ☐ **tie** [táɪ]
- ☐ **rope** [róʊp]

◆KEY SENTENCES (☞ p. 67)

45 When men want to warn others / about danger, / they always send someone / with a big bell.

46 Now, / if the cat wears a bell / around her neck, / it will ring / every time she moves.

The young mouse looked around the room.
The other mice liked his idea.
They thought the plan was perfect!

47 One after another,
the mice stood up to say
something about it.

Three of them spoke about the size
of the bell.

A fourth mouse said
the bell should be gold or silver.

48 A fifth mouse said the rope for the bell
should be a pink or blue color.

他のネズミたちは彼のアイデアを気に入りました。3匹は鈴のサイズについて、4匹目は鈴の材質について、5匹目はひもの色について述べました。

Every mouse talked about the bell and the rope.

(77[1,764] words)

◆KEYWORDS

- ☐ *look around*
- ☐ **plan** [plǽn]
- ☐ **perfect** [pəʳfékt]
- ☐ *one after another*
- ☐ **spoke** [spóʊk] < speak
- ☐ **size** [sáɪz]
- ☐ **should** [ʃʊ́d]
- ☐ **gold** [góʊld]
- ☐ **silver** [sílvəʳ]
- ☐ **pink** [píŋk]

◆KEY SENTENCES (☞ p. 67)

47 One after another, / the mice stood up / to say something / about it.

48 A fifth mouse said / the rope for the bell / should be / a pink or blue color.

Then it was time to make a decision.

Each mouse wrote his opinion
on some paper.

The secretary of the committee
collected all the papers.

49 Then the secretary gave the papers
to the most important mouse
of the committee,
the chairman.

The chairman looked at
every piece of paper.
50 Everyone wrote that they agreed with
the plan of the smart young mouse.

決定の時が来て、それぞれのネズミが意見を紙に書き、書記が集めて議長に渡しました。議長と委員会はアイデアを出した若いネズミに感謝しました。

The chairman and the committee thanked the young mouse for his fine idea.

(75[1,839] words)

◆KEYWORDS

- ☐ **decision** [dɪsíʒən]
- ☐ *make a decision*
- ☐ **opinion** [əpínjən]
- ☐ **paper** [péɪpə^{r}]
- ☐ **secretary** [sékrətèri]
- ☐ **collect** [kəlékt]
- ☐ **gave** [géɪv] < give
- ☐ **important** [ìmpɔ́ː^{r}tənt]
- ☐ **chairman** [tʃéə^{r}mən]
- ☐ **piece** [píːs]
- ☐ *agree with*

◆KEY SENTENCES (☞ p. 67–68)

[49] Then / the secretary gave the papers / to the most important mouse / of the committee, / the chairman.

[50] Everyone wrote / that / they agreed with the plan / of the smart young mouse.

The smart young mouse stood up again.
51 He started to say how pleased he was
with their thanks.

But he was stopped
by a quiet, old, gray mouse
sitting in the corner.

The old mouse looked up and said,
“Yes,
the idea is quite good.

The pink rope and the silver bell
will do nicely.

52 But who will tie the bell
around the neck of the cat?”

(67[1,906] words)

若い利口なネズミが喜んで再び話し始めたとき、隅にいた年を取った灰色のネズミが尋ねました。「しかし、誰がネコの首に鈴をつけるのですか？」

◆ KEYWORDS

- ☐ **corner** [kɔ́ː^{r}nə^{r}]
- ☐ *sit in the corner*
- ☐ *look up*
- ☐ **quite** [kwáɪt]

◆ KEY SENTENCES (☞ p. 68)

51 He started to say / how pleased he was / with their thanks.

52 But / who will tie the bell / around the neck / of the cat?

The meeting became very quiet.
The smart young mouse quickly sat down.

53 “Oh—I—I—well,
I am going to be married!”
he said,
as if that was a good reason
to not tie the bell to the cat.

“But my good friend on my right—”

“I am married!”
cried the friend on the right.
“And my wife is waiting for me!
It’s very late! I must go home!”

Then the chairman stood up
with the secretary.

若い利口なネズミは「私は結婚するつもりです！」とネコに鈴を結ばないよい理由でもあるかのように言いました。議長は会議の終了を宣言しました。

"Hmm!" he said.

"This meeting is now over.
54 The secretary will call
another meeting in a few weeks.

Goodbye,
gentlemen!
Goodbye!"

(99 [2,005] words)

◆KEYWORDS

- ☐ *sit down*
- ☐ *be going to*
- ☐ **married** [mérid]
- ☐ **as** [əz]
- ☐ *as if*
- ☐ **reason** [ríːzən]
- ☐ *on the right*
- ☐ **wife** [wáɪf]
- ☐ **wait** [wéɪt]
- ☐ **must** [mʌ́st]
- ☐ *call a meeting*
- ☐ **few** [fjúː]
- ☐ **gentlemen** [dʒéntəlmɪn]
  < gentleman

◆KEY SENTENCES (☞ p. 68)

53 "Oh—I—I—well, / I am going to be married!" / he said, / as if / that was a good reason / to not tie the bell / to the cat.
54 The secretary will call another meeting / in a few weeks.

And he ran away with the secretary.

Now there was no secretary to take notes.
And there was no chairman to keep order.

So all the other mice decided
to go home too.

At last there was nobody left
but the old, quiet, gray mouse.

He sat there saying to himself:

“A very good idea!
A very good idea!
But who is going to tie the bell
around the cat’s neck?”

(71 [2,076] words)

書記も議長もいなくなり、他のネズミたちはみな家に帰ることにしました。
最後に、年取った、静かな、灰色のネズミだけが残りました。

◆KEYWORDS

☐ *run away*
☐ **note** [nóʊt]
☐ *take notes*
☐ **keep** [kíːp]
☐ **order** [ɔ́ːʳdəʳ]
☐ *keep order*
☐ *at last*
☐ **himself** [hɪmsélf]

◆KEY SENTENCES (☞ p. 68)

55 At last / there was nobody left / but the old, quiet, gray mouse.

〈KEY SENTENCES の訳〉

1. A hare lived high on a mountain near a river.
ウサギは川の近くの山の高いところに住んでいました。

2. One day, the tortoise found the hare staring at him.
ある日、カメはウサギが彼を見つめているのを見つけました。

3. The tortoise tried to show the hare that he had legs.
カメは自分が足を持っていることをウサギに見せようとしました。

4. The tortoise did not like the hare laughing at him.
カメはウサギが彼を笑うのが好きではありませんでした。

5. Mr. Fox over there can be our judge.
あそこにいるキツネさんが、審判をしてくれます。

6. The hare laughed even harder, thinking the tortoise was crazy.
ウサギはカメが狂ったのかと思って、さらに大笑いしました。

7. The course went down the mountain, around the river, and through the woods to a city many miles away.
コースは山を下り、川を回り、森を抜けて何マイルも離れた町へと向かっていました。

8. “That tortoise will not catch up with me,” thought the hare.
「あのカメは追いつかないだろう」とウサギは思いました。

9. “I will sleep here for a little while and then run again in the evening.”
「しばらくの間ここで寝て、夕方にまた走ることにしよう」

10. It took him all afternoon.
午後中ずっとかかりました。

11. And, after walking all day and all night, he was finally close to the city.
そして、一日中、一晩中歩いた後、ようやく彼は町に近づきました。

12. When he saw the morning sun shining, he jumped to his feet.
彼は朝日が輝くのを見たとき、いきなり立ち上がりました。

13. But when he reached the city, what do you think he saw there?
しかし、彼が町に着いたとき、彼はそこで何を見たと思いますか?

14. "He may be slow, but he works hard and never stops to rest."
「彼は遅いかもしれませんが、彼は懸命に働き、休むために止まることはありません」

15. "Working slowly but surely will win the race."
「ゆっくりでも確実に働けばレースに勝つことができます」

16. And many animals lived in this forest, including big wolves.
そして、大きなオオカミを含む多くの動物がこの森に住んでいました。

17. In the summer, there were many animals in the forest and the wolves had lots to eat.
夏になると、森には多くの動物がいて、オオカミはたくさん食べるものがありました。

18. One day, the wolves came out of the forest to look for food.
ある日、オオカミが食べ物を探すために森から出てきました。

19. They walked through the hills where the farmers lived with their sheep.
彼ら(オオカミ)は農民が羊と一緒に住んでいた丘を歩いて通りました。

20. They saw that it worked very well.
彼らはそれが非常に効果的であることを知りました。

21. All they had to do was shout, "Wolf! Wolf!" and every shepherd came to help at any time of day or night.
彼らがしなければならなかったのは、「オオカミ！ オオカミだ！」と叫ぶことだけで、そうするとすべての羊飼いが昼夜を問わずいつでも助けに来ました。

22. He told his son to watch the sheep while he was gone.
彼は息子に、自分が留守の間羊を見張るように言いました。

23. "If you see a wolf, just shout 'Wolf! Wolf!' and the other shepherds will come to help you."
「もしオオカミを見かけたら、『オオカミ！ オオカミだ！』と叫ぶだけで、他の羊飼いたちがお前を助けに来るだろう」

24. The boy asked his father not to go, but the old shepherd had to leave.
少年は父親に行かないように頼みましたが、年老いた羊飼いは出かけなければなりませんでした。

25. So the boy sat next to his sheep, holding his stick in fear.
それで少年は羊の隣に座って、恐怖の中で杖を握っていました。

26. They gathered near the boy, ready to fight the wolves.
彼らは少年の近くに集まり、オオカミと戦う用意ができていました。

27. “What is the matter?” they asked the boy.
「一体どうしたんだ?」と、彼らは少年に尋ねました。

28. “You made us leave our warm beds!” the shepherds said to the boy.
「お前は私たちを暖かいベッドから引っ張り出した!」と羊飼いたちは少年に言いました。

29. “Wolf! Wolf!” came the boy’s voice from across the hills.
「オオカミ! オオカミだ!」丘を越えて少年の声が聞こえてきました。

30. “You are just seeing shadows made by the moon!”
「お前は月によってできた影を見ているだけだ!」

31. How can you think a shadow is a wolf?
どうやったら影がオオカミだと思えるんだ?

32. The shepherds were walking back home when they heard the boy cry out a third time.
羊飼いたちは少年の3回目の叫び声を聞いたとき、彼らは家に引き返してきていました。

33. Saying this, they walked home.
そう言って、彼らは歩いて帰宅しました。

34. But sadly, this time it really was a wolf!
しかし、悲しいことに、今回は本当にオオカミでした!

35. When the boy’s father came home several days later, his son and his sheep were gone.
少年の父親が数日後に帰宅したとき、彼の息子と彼の羊はいなくなっていました。

36. “If you cry ‘wolf’ for shadows, nobody will come to help when a real wolf comes.”
「もし影をオオカミだと叫んだら、本物のオオカミが来たときに誰も助けに来ないだろう」

37. The mill had hundreds of mice living in its walls.
製粉所の壁には何百匹ものネズミが住んでいました。

38. So he walked around to look at it.
それで彼はそれを歩き回って見ました。

39. All the mice took their children and ran quickly up to the next floor.
すべてのネズミは子どもを連れて、すぐに次の階まで走りました。

40. She caught and ate five or six of the fattest mice.
彼女は太ったネズミを5、6匹捕まえて食べました。

41. The biggest problem was that the mice could not hear her.
一番の問題は、ネズミたちには彼女の音を聞くことができないことでした。

42. The mice only saw her big, green eyes when it was too late.
ネズミたちが彼女の大きな緑色の目を見るのは、すでに手遅れになった時でした。

43. They asked the wisest mice in Mouse-town to hold a committee meeting.
彼らはネズミの町で一番賢いネズミに委員会を開くように頼みました。

44. They said they could run and hide if they could hear the cat coming.
彼らはネコが来るのを聞くことができれば走って隠れることができると言いました。

45. When men want to warn others about danger, they always send someone with a big bell.
人間が危険について他の人に警告したいとき、彼らはいつでも大きな鐘を持った誰かを送ります。

46. Now, if the cat wears a bell around her neck, it will ring every time she moves.
今、ネコが首に鈴をつけていれば、ネコが動くたびに鈴が鳴るでしょう。

47. One after another, the mice stood up to say something about it.
次から次へと、ネズミたちは立ち上がってそれについて何か言いました。

48. A fifth mouse said the rope for the bell should be a pink or blue color.
5匹目のネズミは、鈴のロープはピンクまたは青色にする必要があると言いました。

49. Then the secretary gave the papers to the most important mouse of the committee, the chairman.
その後、書記は委員会の最も重要なネズミである議長にその書類を渡しました。

50. Everyone wrote that they agreed with the plan of the smart young mouse.
みんなが、利口な若いネズミの計画に同意すると書きました。

51. He started to say how pleased he was with their thanks.
彼は彼らの感謝にどれほど喜んでいるかを言い始めました。

52. But who will tie the bell around the neck of the cat?
しかし、誰がネコの首に鈴を結ぶのでしょうか？

53. "Oh—I—I—well, I am going to be married!" he said, as if that was a good reason to not tie the bell to the cat.
「ああ……私……私は……まあ、私は結婚するつもりです！」あたかもそれがネコに鈴を結びつけないことのよい理由であるかのように彼は言いました。

54. The secretary will call another meeting in a few weeks.
書記が数週間後にまた会議を招集いたします。

55. At last there was nobody left but the old, quiet, gray mouse.
とうとう、だれもいなくなって、年を取った静かな灰色のネズミだけになりました。

Word List

A
B
C
D
E
F
G
H
I
J
K
L
M
N
O
P
Q
R
S
T
U
V
W
X
Y
Z

・語形が規則変化する語の見出しは原形で示しています。不規則変化語は本文中で使われている形になっています。

・一般的な意味を紹介していますので、一部の語で本文で実際に使われている品詞や意味と合っていないことがあります。

・品詞は以下のように示しています。

名 名詞	代 代名詞	形 形容詞	副 副詞	動 動詞	助 助動詞
前 前置詞	接 接続詞	間 間投詞	冠 冠詞	略 略語	俗 俗語
熟 熟語	頭 接頭語	尾 接尾語	記 記号	関 関係代名詞	

A

□ **a** 冠 ①1つの，1人の，ある ②～につき

□ **able** 形 ①《be – to ～》(人が)～することができる ②能力のある

□ **about** 副 ①およそ，約 ②まわりに，あたりを 前 ①～について ②～のまわりに[の] **speak about** ～について話す

□ **across** 前 ～を渡って，～の向こう側に，(身体の一部に)かけて 副 渡って，向こう側に **run across** 走って渡る

□ **Aesop** 名 イソップ，アイソーポス《イソップ物語(Aesop's Fables)を作ったとされる，古代ギリシャの寓話作家(前620年頃生–前564年頃没)》

□ **Aesop's Fables** イソップ物語《イソップ(Aesop)作とされる，紀元前5世紀の古代ギリシャの寓話集》

□ **afraid** 形 ①心配して ②恐れて，こわがって **be afraid of** ～を恐れる，～を怖がる

□ **after** 前 ①～の後に[で]，～の次に ②《前後に名詞がきて》次々に～，何度も～《反復・継続を表す》 **one after another** 次々に，1つ[人]ずつ 副 後に[で] 接 (～した)後に[で] 動 ～の後を追って，～を捜して

□ **afternoon** 名 午後

□ **again** 副 再び，もう一度 **Not again.** またか，またやってるよ

□ **ago** 副 ～前に

□ **agree** 動 ①同意する ②意見が一致する **agree with** (人)に同意する

□ **all** 形 すべての，～中 **all day** 一日中，明けても暮れても **all over** ～中で，全体に亘って，～の至る所で 代 全部，すべて(のもの[人]) 名 全体 副 まったく，すっかり

□ **alone** 形 ただひとりの 副 ひとりで，～だけで **leave ~ alone** ～を

そっとしておく

□ **along** 前 ～に沿って 副 ～に沿って，前へ，進んで **come along** やって来る，現れる **walk along** (前へ) 歩く，～に沿って歩く

□ **always** 副 いつも，常に

□ **am** 動 ～である，(～に) いる [ある] 《主語がIのときのbeの現在形》

□ **an** 冠 ①1つの，1人の，ある ②～につき

□ **and** 接 ①そして，～と… ②《同じ語を結んで》ますます ③《結果を表して》それで，だから

□ **angry** 形 怒って，腹を立てて

□ **animal** 名 動物 形 動物の

□ **another** 形 ①もう1つ [1人] の ②別の 代 ①もう1つ [1人] ②別のもの **one after another** 次々に，1つ [人] ずつ **one another** お互い

□ **any** 形 ①《疑問文で》何か，いくつかの ②《否定文で》何も，少しも (～ない) ③《肯定文で》どの～も **any time** いつでも **at any time of day or night** 昼夜を問わずいつでも 代 ①《疑問文で》(～のうち) 何か，どれか，誰か ②《否定文で》少しも，何も [誰も] ～ない ③《肯定文で》どれも，誰でも

□ **anything** 代 ①《疑問文で》何か，どれでも ②《否定文で》何も，どれも (～ない) ③《肯定文で》何でも，どれでも **anything else** ほかの何か 副 いくらか

□ **are** 動 ～である，(～に) いる [ある] 《主語がyou, we, theyまたは複数名詞のときのbeの現在形》

□ **around** 副 ①まわりに，あちこちに ②およそ，約 **look around** まわりを見回す **walk around** 歩き回る，ぶらぶら歩く 前 ～のまわりに，～のあちこちに

□ **arrogant** 形 尊大な，傲慢な，無礼な，横柄な

□ **as** 接 ①《as ～ as …の形で》…と同じくらい～ ②～のとおりに，～のように ③～しながら，～しているときに ④～するにつれて，～にしたがって ⑤～なので ⑥～だけれども ⑦～する限りでは 前 ①～として (の) ②～の時 **as if** あたかも～のように，まるで～みたいに 副 同じくらい 代 ①～のような ②～だが

□ **ask** 動 ①尋ねる，聞く ②頼む，求める

□ **asleep** 形 眠って (いる状態の) 副 眠って，休止して

□ **at** 前 ①《場所・時》～に [で] ②《目標・方向》～に [を]，～に向かって ③《原因・理由》～を見て [聞いて・知って] ④～に従事して，～の状態で **at any time of day or night** 昼夜を問わずいつでも **at last** ついに，とうとう **late at night** 夜遅くに

□ **ate** 動 eat (食べる) の過去

□ **away** 副 離れて，遠くに，去って，わきに **chase away** ～を追い払う **go away** 立ち去る **run away** 走り去る，逃げ出す **walk away** 立ち去る，遠ざかる 形 離れた，遠征した

B

□ **back** 名 ①背中 ②裏，後ろ

副 ①戻って ②後ろへ[に] come back 戻る 形 裏の, 後ろの

□ **be** 動 ～である, (～に)いる[ある], ～となる **be afraid of** ～を恐れる, ～を怖がる **be close to** ～に近い 助 ①《現在分詞とともに用いて》～している ②《過去分詞とともに用いて》～される, ～されている

□ **became** 動 become (なる) の過去

□ **because** 接 (なぜなら) ～だから, ～という理由[原因]で

□ **become** 動 ①(～に)なる ②(～に)似合う ③becomeの過去分詞

□ **bed** 名 ①ベッド, 寝所 ②花壇, 川床, 土台 **go to bed** 床につく, 寝る

□ **behind** 前 ①～の後ろに, ～の背後に ②～に遅れて, ～に劣って 副 ①後ろに, 背後に ②遅れて, 劣って **far behind** かなり遅れて

□ **believe** 動 信じる, 信じている, (～と)思う, 考える

□ **bell** 名 ベル, 鈴, 鐘 動 ①(ベル・鐘が)鳴る ②ベル[鈴]をつける

□ **big** 形 ①大きい ②偉い, 重要な 副 ①大きく, 大いに ②自慢して

□ **blue** 形 ①青い ②青ざめた ③憂うつな, 陰気な 名 青(色)

□ **body** 名 体, 死体, 胴体

□ **boy** 名 ①少年, 男の子 ②給仕

□ **brother** 名 ①兄弟 ②同僚, 同胞

□ **but** 接 ①でも, しかし ②～を除いて 前 ～を除いて, ～のほかは 副 ただ, のみ, ほんの

□ **by** 前 ①《位置》～のそばに[で] ②《手段・方法・行為者・基準》～によって, ～で ③《期限》～までには ④《通過・経由》～を経由して, ～を通って **by one's side** ～の近くに 副 そばに, 通り過ぎて

C

□ **call** 動 ①呼ぶ, 叫ぶ ②電話をかける ③立ち寄る **call a meeting** 会議を招集する **call for** ～を求める, ～を呼び求める, 呼び出す **call for help** 助けを求めて呼ぶ

□ **came** 動 come (来る) の過去

□ **can** 助 ①～できる ②～してもよい ③～でありうる ④《否定文で》～のはずがない **How can you** どうして～できるのか

□ **cat** 名 ネコ(猫)

□ **catch** 動 ①つかまえる ②追いつく ③(病気に)かかる **catch up with** ～に追いつく

□ **caught** 動 catch (つかまえる) の過去, 過去分詞

□ **chairman** 名 委員長, 会長, 議長

□ **chase** 動 ①追跡する, 追い[探し]求める ②追い立てる **chase away** ～を追い払う

□ **child** 名 子ども

□ **children** 名 child (子ども) の複数

□ **city** 名 ①都市, 都会 ②《the –》(全)市民

□ **close** 形 ①近い ②親しい ③狭い **be close to** ～に近い 副 ①接近して ②密集して 動 ①閉まる, 閉める ②終える, 閉店する

□ **cold** 形 ①寒い, 冷たい ②冷淡な, 冷静な 名 ①寒さ, 冷たさ ②風邪

□ **collect** 動 ①集める, 集金する ②まとめる

□ **color** 名 ①色, 色彩 ②絵の具 ③血色 動 色をつける

□ **come** 動 ①来る, 行く, 現れる ②(出来事が)起こる, 生じる ③～になる ④comeの過去分詞 **come along** やって来る, 現れる **come back** 戻る **come out of** ～から出てくる **come up** 近づいてくる, 浮上する, 水面へ上ってくる

□ **committee** 名 委員(会), 評議会

□ **corner** 名 ①曲がり角, 角 ②すみ, はずれ **sit in the corner** 〔部屋の〕隅に座る 動 ①窮地に追いやる ②買い占める ③角を曲がる

□ **could** 助 ①can(～できる)の過去 ②《控え目な推量・可能性・願望などを表す》

□ **course** 名 ①進路, 方向 ②経過, 成り行き ③科目, 講座 ④策, 方策 **of course** もちろん, 当然

□ **coward** 名 臆病者 形 勇気のない, 臆病な

□ **crazy** 形 ①狂気の, ばかげた, 無茶な ②夢中の, 熱狂的な

□ **cross** 動 ①横切る, 渡る ②じゃまする ③十字を切る

□ **cry** 動 泣く, 叫ぶ, 大声を出す, 嘆く **cry out** 叫ぶ 名 泣き声, 叫び, かっさい

D

□ **danger** 名 危険, 障害, 脅威

□ **day** 名 ①日中, 昼間 ②日, 期日 ③《-s》時代, 生涯 **all day** 一日中, 明けても暮れても **at any time of day or night** 昼夜を問わずいつでも **every day** 毎日 **In a day or two** 一両日中に **one day** (過去の)ある日, (未来の)いつか

□ **decide** 動 決定[決意]する, (～しようと)決める, 判決を下す **decide to do** ～することに決める

□ **decision** 名 ①決定, 決心 ②判決 **make a decision** 決定する

□ **did** 動 do(～をする)の過去 助 doの過去

□ **disappear** 動 見えなくなる, 姿を消す, なくなる

□ **do** 助 ①《ほかの動詞とともに用いて現在形の否定文・疑問文をつくる》 ②《同じ動詞を繰り返す代わりに用いる》 ③《動詞を強調するのに用いる》 動 ～をする **decide to do** ～することに決める **need to do** ～する必要がある **start to do** ～し始める

□ **down** 副 ①下へ, 降りて, 低くなって ②倒れて **go down** 下に降りる **lie down** 横たわる, 横になる **look down** 見下ろす **run down** 駆け下りる **sit down** 座る, 着席する 前 ～の下方へ, ～を下って 形 下方の, 下りの

E

□ **each** 形 それぞれの, 各自の

each other お互いに 代それぞれ，各自 副それぞれに

□ **easy** 形 ①やさしい，簡単な ②気楽な，くつろいだ

□ **eat** 動食べる，食事する

□ **else** 副 ①そのほかに［の］，代わりに ②さもないと **anything else** ほかの何か

□ **even** 副 ①《強意》～でさえも，～ですら，いっそう，なおさら ②平等に **even though** ～であるけれども，～にもかかわらず

□ **evening** 名 ①夕方，晩 ②《the［one's］－》末期，晩年，衰退期

□ **every** 形 ①どの～も，すべての，あらゆる ②毎～，～ごとの **every day** 毎日 **every time** ～するときはいつも

□ **everyone** 代誰でも，皆

□ **eye** 名 ①目，視力 ②眼識，観察力 ③注目

F

□ **fable** 名寓話

□ **face** 名顔，顔つき

□ **family** 名家族，家庭，一門，家柄

□ **far** 副 ①遠くに，はるかに，離れて ②《比較級を強めて》ずっと，はるかに **far behind** かなり遅れて 形遠い，向こうの 名遠方

□ **farmer** 名農民，農場経営者

□ **fast** 形 ①（速度が）速い ②（時計が）進んでいる ③しっかりした 副 ①速く，急いで ②（時計が）進んで ③しっかりと，ぐっすりと

□ **fat** 形 ①太った ②脂っこい ③分厚い 名脂肪，肥満

□ **father** 名父親

□ **fear** 名 ①恐れ ②心配，不安 **in fear** おどおどして，ビクビクして 動 ①恐れる ②心配する

□ **feel** 動感じる，～と思う

□ **feet** 名 ①foot（足）の複数 ②フィート《長さの単位。約30cm》 **jump to one's feet** 飛び起きる

□ **felt** 動feel（感じる）の過去，過去分詞

□ **few** 形 ①ほとんどない，少数の（～しかない） ②《a－》少数の，少しはある 代少数の人［物］

□ **fifth** 名第5番目（の人［物］），5日 形第5番目の

□ **fight** 動（～と）戦う，争う 名 ①戦い，争い，けんか ②闘志，ファイト

□ **finally** 副最後に，ついに，結局

□ **find** 動 ①見つける ②（～と）わかる，気づく，～と考える ③得る **find out** 見つけ出す，気がつく

□ **fine** 形 ①元気な ②美しい，りっぱな，申し分ない，結構な ③晴れた ④細かい，微妙な 副りっぱに，申し分なく

□ **finish** 動終わる，終える 名終わり，最後

□ **finish line** （競争の）ゴール

□ **five** 名5（の数字），5人［個］ 形5の，5人［個］の

□ **flat** 形 ①平らな ②しぼんだ，空気の抜けた 副 ①平らに，平たく ②きっかり

□ **floor** 名床，階

□ **food** 名食物，えさ，肥料

□ **foolish** 形おろかな，ばかばかしい

□ **for** 前①《目的・原因・対象》～にとって，～のために[の]，～に対して ②《期間》～間 ③《代理》～の代わりに ④《方向》～へ（向かって） **call for** ～を求める，～を呼び求める，呼び出す **call for help** 助けを求めて呼ぶ **for a while** しばらく（の間），少しの間 **for ～ years** ～年間，～年にわたって **look for** ～を探す **thank ～ for** ～に対して礼を言う **wait for** ～を待つ 接というわけは～，なぜなら～，だから

□ **forest** 名森林

□ **found** 動①find（見つける）の過去，過去分詞 ②～の基礎を築く，～を設立する

□ **fourth** 名第4番目（の人・物），4日 形第4番目の

□ **fox** 名キツネ（狐）

□ **friend** 名友だち，仲間

□ **from** 前①《出身・出発点・時間・順序・原料》～から ②《原因・理由》～がもとで

□ **funny** 形①おもしろい，こっけいな ②奇妙な，うさんくさい

G

□ **gather** 動①集まる，集める ②生じる，増す ③推測する

□ **gave** 動give（与える）の過去

□ **gentleman** 名紳士

□ **gentlemen** 名gentleman（紳士）の複数

□ **give** 動与える，贈る

□ **go** 動①行く，出かける ②動く ③進む，経過する，いたる ④（ある状態に）なる **be going to** ～するつもりである **go away** 立ち去る **go down** 下に降りる **go home** 帰宅する **go to bed** 床につく，寝る

□ **gold** 名金，金貨，金製品，金色 形金の，金製の，金色の

□ **gone** 動go（行く）の過去分詞 形去った，使い果たした，死んだ

□ **good** 形①よい，上手な，優れた，美しい ②（数量・程度が）かなりの，相当な

□ **goodbye** 間さようなら 名別れのあいさつ

□ **grain** 名①穀物，穀類，（穀物の）粒 ②粒，極少量 動粒にする

□ **grass** 名草，牧草（地），芝生 動草[芝生]で覆う[覆われる]

□ **grave** 名墓 形重要な，厳粛な，落ち着いた

□ **gray** 形①灰色の ②どんよりした，憂うつな ③白髪の 名灰色 動灰色になる[する]

□ **green** 形①緑色の，青々とした ②未熟な，若い ③生き生きした 名①緑色 ②草地，芝生，野菜

H

□ **had** 動have（持つ）の過去，過去分詞 助haveの過去《過去完了の文をつくる》

□ **happen** 動 ①(出来事が)起こる, 生じる ②偶然[たまたま] ～する

□ **happy** 形 幸せな, うれしい, 幸運な, 満足して

□ **hard** 形 ①堅い ②激しい, むずかしい ③熱心な, 勤勉な ④無情な, 耐えがたい, 厳しい, きつい
副 ①一生懸命に ②激しく ③堅く

□ **hare** 名 野ウサギ

□ **have** 動 ①持つ, 持っている, 抱く ②(～が)ある, いる ③食べる, 飲む ④経験する, (病気に)かかる ⑤催す, 開く ⑥(人に) ～させる **have to** ～しなければならない 助《〈have＋過去分詞〉の形で現在完了の文をつくる》～した, ～したことがある, ずっと～している

□ **he** 代 彼は[が]

□ **head** 名 ①頭 ②先頭 ③長, 指導者 **shake one's head**〔疑念・落胆・恥ずかしさなどを表すために〕頭[首]を横[左右]に振る 動 向かう, 向ける

□ **hear** 動 聞く, 聞こえる

□ **heard** 動 hear(聞く)の過去, 過去分詞

□ **held** 動 hold(つかむ)の過去, 過去分詞

□ **help** 動 ①助ける, 手伝う ②給仕する 名 助け, 手伝い **call for help** 助けを求めて呼ぶ

□ **her** 代 ①彼女を[に] ②彼女の

□ **here** 副 ①ここに[で] ②《－is [are] ～》ここに～がある ③さあ, そら 名 ここ

□ **hid** 動 hide(隠れる)の過去, 過去分詞

□ **hide** 動 隠れる, 隠す, 隠れて見えない, 秘密にする

□ **high** 形 ①高い ②気高い, 高価な 副 ①高く ②ぜいたくに 名 高い所

□ **hill** 名 丘, 塚

□ **him** 代 彼を[に]

□ **himself** 代 彼自身

□ **his** 代 ①彼の ②彼のもの

□ **hmm** 間 ふむ, ううむ《熟考・疑問・ためらいなどを表す》

□ **hold** 動 ①つかむ, 持つ, 抱く ②保つ, 持ちこたえる ③収納できる, 入れることができる ④(会などを)開く **hold a meeting** 会議を開く 名 ①つかむこと, 保有 ②支配[理解]力

□ **home** 名 ①家, 自国, 故郷, 家庭 ②収容所 副 家に, 自国へ **go home** 帰宅する 形 家の, 家庭の, 地元の

□ **how** 副 ①どうやって, どれくらい, どんなふうに ②なんて(～だろう) ③《関係副詞》～する方法 **How can you** どうして～できるのか

□ **hundred** 名 ①100(の数字), 100人[個] ②《-s》何百, 多数 **hundreds of** 何百もの～
形 ①100の, 100人[個]の ②多数の

□ **hungry** 形 ①空腹の, 飢えた ②渇望して ③不毛の

□ **hunt** 動 狩る, 狩りをする, 探し求める 名 狩り, 追跡

□ **hunter** 名 ①狩りをする人, 狩人, ハンター ②猟馬, 猟犬

I

□ **I** 代 私は[が]

□ **idea** 名 考え, 意見, アイデア, 計画

□ **if** 接 もし～ならば, たとえ～でも, ～かどうか **as if** あたかも～のように, まるで～みたいに 名 疑問, 条件, 仮定

□ **important** 形 重要な, 大切な, 有力な

□ **in** 前 ①《場所・位置・所属》～(の中)に[で・の] ②《時》～(の時)に[の・で], ～後(に), ～の間(に) ③《方法・手段》～で ④～を身につけて, ～を着て ⑤～に関して, ～について ⑥《状態》～の状態で **In a day or two** 一両日中に **in fear** おどおどして, ビクビクして **sit in the corner** 〔部屋の〕隅に座る 副 中へ[に], 内へ[に]

□ **include** 動 含む, 勘定に入れる

□ **including** 前 ～を含む, ～などの

□ **is** 動 be(～である)の3人称単数現在

□ **it** 代 ①それは[が], それを[に] ②《天候・日時・距離・寒暖などを示す》

□ **its** 代 それの, あれの

J

□ **judge** 動 判決を下す, 裁く, 判断する, 評価する 名 裁判官, 判事, 審査員

□ **jump** 動 ①跳ぶ, 跳躍する, 飛び越える, 飛びかかる ②(～を)熱心にやり始める **jump out of** ～から飛び出す **jump to one's feet** 飛び起きる **jump up** 素早く立ち上がる 名 ①跳躍 ②急騰, 急転

□ **just** 形 正しい, もっともな, 当然な 副 ①まさに, ちょうど, (～した)ばかり ②ほんの, 単に, ただ～だけ ③ちょっと

K

□ **keep** 動 ①とっておく, 保つ, 続ける ②(～を…に)しておく ③飼う, 養う ④経営する ⑤守る **keep order** 秩序を保つ

□ **kept** 動 keep(とっておく)の過去, 過去分詞

□ **kill** 動 殺す, 消す, 枯らす 名 殺すこと

□ **know** 動 ①知っている, 知る, (～が)わかる, 理解している ②知り合いである

L

□ **lake** 名 湖, 湖水, 池

□ **last** 形 ①《the –》最後の ②この前の, 先～ ③最新の 副 ①最後に ②この前 名《the –》最後(のもの), 終わり **at last** ついに, とうとう

□ **late** 形 ①遅い, 後期の ②最近の ③《the –》故～ 副 ①遅れて, 遅く ②最近まで, 以前 **late at night** 夜遅くに

□ **later** 形 もっと遅い, もっと後の 副 後で, 後ほど

A B C D E F G H I J K L M N O P Q R S T U V W X Y Z

□ **laugh** 動笑う 名笑い(声)

□ **lay** 動 ①置く, 横たえる, 敷く ②整える ③卵を産む ④lie(横たわる)の過去

□ **leave** 動 ①出発する, 去る ②残す, 置き忘れる ③(～を…の)ままにしておく ④ゆだねる **leave ～ alone** ～をそっとしておく 名 ①休暇 ②許可 ③別れ

□ **left** 動leave(去る, ～をあとに残す)の過去, 過去分詞

□ **leg** 名 ①脚, すね ②支柱

□ **let** 動(人に～)させる, (～するのを)許す, (～をある状態に)する **let us** どうか私たちに～させてください

□ **lie** 動 ①横たわる, 寝る ②(ある状態に)ある, 存在する

□ **lie down** 横たわる, 横になる

□ **like** 動好む, 好きである 前 ～に似ている, ～のような **look like** ～のように見える **nothing like** 《be ～》 ～とはまるで違っている 形似ている, ～のような 接あたかも～のように

□ **line** 名 ①線, 糸, 電話線 ②(字の)行 ③列, (電車の) ～線 **finish line** (競争の)ゴール 動 ①線を引く ②整列する

□ **little** 形 ①小さい, 幼い ②少しの, 短い ③ほとんど～ない, 《a－》少しはある 名少し(しか), 少量 副全然～ない, 《a－》少しはある

□ **live** 動住む, 暮らす, 生きている 形 ①生きている, 生きた ②ライブの, 実況の

□ **long** 形 ①長い, 長期の ②《長さ・距離・時間などを示す語句を伴って》 ～の長さ[距離・時間]の 副長い間, ずっと 名長い期間

□ **look** 動 ①見る ②(～に)見える, (～の)顔つきをする ③注意する ④《間投詞のように》ほら, ねえ **look around** まわりを見回す **look down** 見下ろす **look for** ～を探す **look like** ～のように見える **look up** 見上げる 名 ①一見, 目つき ②外観, 外見, 様子

□ **lose** 動 ①失う, 迷う, 忘れる ②負ける, 失敗する

□ **lost** 動lose(負ける)の過去, 過去分詞 形 ①失った, 負けた ②道に迷った, 困った ③没頭している

□ **lot** 名 ①くじ, 運 ②地所, 区画 ③たくさん, たいへん, 《a－of ～/-s of ～》たくさんの～ ④やつ, 連中

M

□ **made** 動make(作る)の過去, 過去分詞 形作った, 作られた

□ **make** 動 ①作る, 得る ②行う, (～に)なる ③(～を…に)する, (～を…)させる **make a decision** 決定する

□ **many** 形多数の, たくさんの 代多数(の人・物)

□ **marker** 名墓碑

□ **married** 動marry(結婚する)の過去, 過去分詞 形結婚した, 既婚の

□ **matter** 名物, 事, 事件, 問題 動《主に疑問文・否定文で》重要である

□ **may** 助 ①～かもしれない ②～してもよい，～できる

□ **me** 代 私を［に］

□ **meanwhile** 副 それまでの間，一方では

□ **meeting** 動 meet（会う）の現在分詞 名 ①集まり，ミーティング，面会 ②競技会 **call a meeting** 会議を招集する **hold a meeting** 会議を開く

□ **men** 名 man（男性）の複数

□ **mice** 名 mouse（ネズミ）の複数

□ **mile** 名 ①マイル《長さの単位。1,609m》 ②《-s》かなりの距離

□ **mill** 名 ①製造所 ②ミル，ひき機 動 ひく

□ **miller** 名 粉屋

□ **mind** 名 ①心，精神，考え ②知性 動 ①気にする，いやがる ②気をつける，用心する

□ **moon** 名 月，月光

□ **morning** 名 朝，午前

□ **most** 形 ①最も多い ②たいていの，大部分の 代 ①大部分，ほとんど ②最多数，最大限 副 最も（多く）

□ **mountain** 名 ①山 ②《the ～ M-s》～山脈 ③山のようなもの，多量

□ **mouse** 名（ハツカ）ネズミ

□ **Mouse-town** ネズミの町

□ **move** 動 ①動く，動かす ②感動させる ③引っ越す，移動する 名 ①動き，運動 ②転居，移動

□ **Mr.** 名《男性に対して》～さん，～氏，～先生

□ **must** 助 ①～しなければならない ②～に違いない 名 絶対に必要なこと［もの］

□ **my** 代 私の

N

□ **near** 前 ～の近くに，～のそばに 形 近い，親しい 副 近くに，親密で

□ **neck** 名 首，（衣服の）えり

□ **need** 動（～を）必要とする，必要である 助 ～する必要がある **need to do** ～する必要がある

□ **neighbor** 名 隣人，隣り合うもの

□ **never** 副 決して［少しも］～ない，一度も［二度と］～ない

□ **next** 形 ①次の，翌～ ②隣の **next time** 次回は **next to** ～のとなりに，～の次に 副 ①次に ②隣に 代 次の人［もの］

□ **nice** 形 すてきな，よい，きれいな，親切な

□ **nicely** 副 ①うまく，よく ②上手に，親切に，几帳面に

□ **night** 名 夜，晩 **at any time of day or night** 昼夜を問わずいつでも **late at night** 夜遅くに

□ **no** 副 ①いいえ，いや ②少しも～ない 形 ～がない，少しも～ない，～どころでない，～禁止 名 否定，拒否

□ **nobody** 代 誰も［1人も］～ない

□ **noise** 名 騒音，騒ぎ，物音

□ **not** 副 ～でない，～しない

□ **Not again.** またか，またやってるよ

□ **note** 名 ①メモ, 覚え書き ②注釈 ③注意, 注目 **take notes** 記録[メモ]を取る 動 ①書き留める ②注意[注目]する

□ **nothing** 代 何も～ない[しない] **nothing like** 《be ～》～とはまるで違っている

□ **now** 副 ①今(では), 現在 ②今すぐに ③では, さて 名 今, 現在 形 今の, 現在の

O

□ **of** 前 ①《所有・所属・部分》～の, ～に属する ②《性質・特徴・材料》～の, ～製の ③《部分》～のうち ④《分離・除去》～から **at any time of day or night** 昼夜を問わずいつでも **be afraid of** ～を恐れる, ～を怖がる **come out of** ～から出てくる **hundreds of** 何百もの～ **jump out of** ～から飛び出す **on top of** ～の上(部)に **one of** ～の1つ[人]

□ **oh** 間 ああ, おや, まあ

□ **old** 形 ①年取った, 老いた ②～歳の ③古い, 昔の 名 昔, 老人

□ **on** 前 ①《場所・接触》～(の上)に ②《日・時》～に, ～と同時に, ～のすぐ後で ③《関係・従事》～に関して, ～について, ～して **on the right** 右[右側]に **on top of** ～の上(部)に **sit on** ～の上に乗る 副 ①身につけて, 上に ②前へ, 続けて

□ **one** 名 1(の数字), 1人[個] **one of** ～の1つ[人] 形 ①1の, 1人[個]の ②ある～ ③《the－》唯一の **one day** (過去の)ある日, (未来の)いつか 代 ①(一般の)人, ある物 ②一方, 片方 ③～なもの **by one's side** ～の近くに **jump to one's feet** 飛び起きる **one after another** 次々に, 1つ[人]ずつ **one another** お互い **shake one's head** 〔疑念・落胆・恥ずかしさなどを表すために〕頭[首]を横[左右]に振る

□ **oneself** 熟 **say to oneself** ひとり言を言う, 心に思う

□ **only** 形 唯一の 副 ①単に, ～にすぎない, ただ～だけ ②やっと 接 ただし, だがしかし

□ **opinion** 名 意見, 見識, 世論, 評判

□ **or** 接 ①～か…, または ②さもないと ③すなわち, 言い換えると **In a day or two** 一両日中に **at any time of day or night** 昼夜を問わずいつでも

□ **order** 名 ①順序 ②整理, 整頓 ③命令, 注文(品) **keep order** 秩序を保つ 動 ①(～するよう)命じる, 注文する ②整頓する, 整理する

□ **other** 形 ①ほかの, 異なった ②(2つのうち)もう一方の, (3つ以上のうち)残りの 代 ①ほかの人[物] ②《the－》残りの1つ **each other** お互いに 副 そうでなく, 別に

□ **our** 代 私たちの

□ **out** 副 ①外へ[に], 不在で, 離れて ②世に出て ③消えて ④すっかり **come out of** ～から出てくる **cry out** 叫ぶ **find out** 見つけ出す, 気がつく **jump out of** ～から飛び

出す stretch out 手足を伸ばす，背伸びする 形 ①外の，遠く離れた ②公表された 前 ～から外へ[に]

□ **over** 前 ①～の上の[に]，～を一面に覆って ②～を越えて，～以上に，～よりまさって ③～の向こう側の[に] ④～の間 **all over** ～中で，全体に亘って，～の至る所で **over there** あそこに 副 上に，一面に，ずっと 形 ①上部の，上位の，過多の ②終わって，すんで

P

□ **paper** 名 ①紙 ②新聞，論文，答案 ③《-s》書類

□ **perfect** 形 ①完璧な，完全な ②純然たる 動 完成する，改良[改善]する

□ **pick** 動 ①(花・果実などを)摘む，もぐ ②選ぶ，精選する ③つつく，つついて穴をあける，ほじくり出す ④(～を)摘み取る **pick up** 拾い上げる

□ **piece** 名 ①一片，部分 ②1個，1本 ③作品

□ **pink** 形 ピンク色の 名 ピンク色

□ **place** 名 ①場所，建物 ②余地，空間 ③《one's -》家，部屋 動 ①置く，配置する ②任命する，任じる

□ **plan** 名 計画，設計(図)，案 動 計画する

□ **pleased** 動 please(喜ばす)の過去，過去分詞 形 喜んだ，気に入った

□ **problem** 名 問題，難問

□ **protect** 動 保護する，防ぐ

Q

□ **quickly** 副 敏速に，急いで

□ **quiet** 形 ①静かな，穏やかな，じっとした ②おとなしい，無口な，目立たない 名 静寂，平穏 動 静まる，静める

□ **quite** 副 ①まったく，すっかり，完全に ②かなり，ずいぶん ③ほとんど

R

□ **race** 名 ①競争，競走 ②人種，種族 動 ①競争[競走]する ②疾走する

□ **ran** 動 run(走る)の過去

□ **reach** 動 ①着く，到着する，届く ②手を伸ばして取る 名 手を伸ばすこと，(手の)届く範囲

□ **ready** 形 用意[準備]ができた，まさに～しようとする，今にも～せんばかりの 動 用意[準備]する **ready to** いつでも～できる，～する心構えができている

□ **real** 形 実際の，実在する，本物の 副 本当に

□ **really** 副 本当に，実際に，確かに

□ **reason** 名 ①理由 ②理性，道理 動 ①推論する ②説き伏せる

□ **remember** 動 思い出す，覚えている，忘れないでいる

□ **rest** 名 ①休息 ②安静 ③休止，

停止 ④《the –》残り 動 ①休む, 眠る ②休止する, 静止する ③(～に)基づいている ④(～の)ままである

□ **return** 動 帰る, 戻る, 返す

□ **right** 形 ①正しい ②適切な ③健全な ④右(側)の 副 ①まっすぐに, すぐに ②右(側)に ③ちょうど, 正確に 名 ①正しいこと ②権利 ③《the –》右 **on the right** 右[右側]に

□ **ring** 動 ①輪で取り囲む ②鳴る, 鳴らす ③電話をかける 名 ①輪, 円形, 指輪 ②競技場, リング

□ **river** 名 ①川 ②(溶岩などの)大量流出

□ **road** 名 ①道路, 道, 通り ②手段, 方法

□ **room** 名 ①部屋 ②空間, 余地

□ **rope** 名 綱, なわ, ロープ 動 なわで縛る

□ **run** 動 ①走る ②運行する ③(川が)流れる ④経営する **run across** 走って渡る **run away** 走り去る, 逃げ出す **run down** 駆け下りる **run through** 走り抜ける **run up** ～に走り寄る 名 ①走ること, 競走 ②連続, 続き ③得点

S

□ **sadly** 副 悲しそうに, 不幸にも

□ **said** 動 say(言う)の過去, 過去分詞

□ **same** 形 ①同じ, 同様の ②前述の 代《the –》同一の人[物] 副《the –》同様に

□ **sat** 動 sit(座る)の過去, 過去分詞

□ **saw** 動 see(見る)の過去

□ **say** 動 言う, 口に出す **say to oneself** ひとり言を言う, 心に思う 名 言うこと, 言い分 間 さあ, まあ

□ **secretary** 名 ①秘書, 書記 ②《S-》長官, 大臣 ③(本箱などのついた)書き物机

□ **see** 動 ①見る, 見える, 見物する ②(～と)わかる, 認識する, 経験する ③会う ④考える, 確かめる, 調べる ⑤気をつける

□ **send** 動 ①送る, 届ける ②手紙を出す ③(人を～に)行かせる ④《– ＋人[物など]＋～ing》～を(ある状態に)する

□ **several** 形 ①いくつかの ②めいめいの 代 いくつかのもの, 数人, 数個

□ **shadow** 名 ①影, 暗がり ②亡霊 動 ①陰にする, 暗くする ②尾行する

□ **shake** 動 ①振る, 揺れる, 揺さぶる, 震える ②動揺させる **shake one's head** 〔疑念・落胆・恥ずかしさなどを表すために〕頭[首]を横[左右]に振る

□ **she** 代 彼女は[が]

□ **sheep** 名 羊

□ **shell** 名 ①貝がら, (木の実・卵などの)から ②(建物の)骨組み

□ **shepherd** 名 ①羊飼い ②牧師 動 (羊の)番をする, 導く

□ **shine** 動 ①光る, 輝く ②光らせる, 磨く 名 光, 輝き

□ **shook** 動 shake(振る)の過去

□ **short** 形 ①短い ②背の低い ③不足している

□ **should** 助 ～すべきである, ～したほうがよい

□ **shout** 動 叫ぶ, 大声で言う, どなりつける 名 叫び, 大声, 悲鳴

□ **show** 動 ①見せる, 示す, 見える ②明らかにする, 教える ③案内する 名 ①表示, 見世物, ショー ②外見, 様子

□ **side** 名 側, 横, そば, 斜面 **by one's side** ～の近くに 形 ①側面の, 横の ②副次的な 動 (～の) 側につく, 賛成する

□ **silver** 名 銀, 銀貨, 銀色 形 銀製の

□ **single** 形 ①たった1つの ②1人用の, それぞれの ③独身の ④片道の

□ **sister** 名 ①姉妹, 姉, 妹 ②修道女

□ **sit** 動 ①座る, 腰掛ける ②止まる ③位置する **sit down** 座る, 着席する **sit in the corner** 〔部屋の〕隅に座る **sit on** ～の上に乗る

□ **six** 名 6 (の数字), 6人 [個] 形 6の, 6人 [個] の

□ **size** 名 大きさ, 寸法, サイズ 動 (大きさに従って) 分類する, 測る

□ **sleep** 動 ①眠る, 寝る ②活動しない 名 ①睡眠, 冬眠 ②静止, 不活動

□ **sleepy** 形 ①眠い, 眠そうな ②活気のない

□ **slow** 形 遅い 副 遅く, ゆっくりと 動 遅くする, 速度を落とす

□ **slowly** 副 遅く, ゆっくり

□ **small** 形 ①小さい, 少ない ②取るに足りない 副 小さく, 細かく

□ **smart** 形 ①利口な, 抜け目のない ②きちんとした, 洗練された ③激しい, ずきずきする

□ **smile** 動 微笑する, にっこり笑う 名 微笑, ほほえみ

□ **so** 副 ①とても ②同様に, ～もまた ③《先行する句・節の代用》そのように, そう 接 ①だから, それで ②では, さて

□ **some** 形 ①いくつかの, 多少の ②ある, 誰か, 何か 副 約, およそ 代 ①いくつか ②ある人 [物] たち

□ **someone** 代 ある人, 誰か

□ **something** 代 ①ある物, 何か ②いくぶん, 多少

□ **son** 名 息子, 子弟, ～の子

□ **soon** 副 まもなく, すぐに, すみやかに

□ **speak** 動 話す, 言う, 演説する **speak about** ～について話す

□ **spoke** 動 speak (話す) の過去

□ **stand** 動 立つ, 立っている, ある **stand up** 立ち上がる

□ **stare** 動 じっと [じろじろ] 見る 名 じっと見ること, 凝視

□ **start** 動 ①出発する, 始まる, 始める ②生じる, 生じさせる **start to do** ～し始める 名 出発, 開始

□ **step** 名 ①歩み, 1歩 (の距離) ②段階 ③踏み段, 階段 動 歩む, 踏む

□ **stick** 名 棒, 杖

□ **still** 副 ①まだ, 今でも ②それでも (なお) 形 静止した, 静かな

□ **stone** 名 ①石, 小石 ②宝石 形 石の, 石製の

□ **stood** 動 stand (立つ) の過去, 過去分詞

□ **stop** 動 ①やめる, やめさせる, 止める, 止まる ②立ち止まる **stop to** ～しようと立ち止まる 名 ①停止 ②停留所, 駅

□ **stretch** 動 引き伸ばす, 広がる, 広げる **stretch out** 手足を伸ばす, 背伸びする 名 ①伸ばす [伸びる] こと, 広がり ②ストレッチ (運動)

□ **stupid** 形 ばかな, おもしろくない

□ **suddenly** 副 突然, 急に

□ **summer** 名 夏

□ **sun** 名《the –》太陽, 日

□ **sure** 形 確かな, 確実な,《be – to ～》必ず [きっと] ～する, 確信して 副 確かに, まったく, 本当に

□ **surely** 副 確かに, きっと

□ **swam** 動 swim (泳ぐ) の過去

T

□ **take** 動 ①取る, 持つ ②持って [連れて] いく, 捕らえる ③乗る ④ (時間・労力を) 費やす, 必要とする ⑤ (ある動作を) する ⑥飲む ⑦耐える, 受け入れる **take notes** 記録 [メモ] を取る 名 ①取得 ②捕獲

□ **talk** 動 話す, 語る, 相談する 名 ①話, おしゃべり ②演説 ③《the –》話題

□ **tell** 動 ①話す, 言う, 語る ②教える, 知らせる, 伝える ③わかる, 見分ける **tell ～ to …** ～に…するように言う

□ **than** 接 ～よりも, ～以上に

□ **thank** 動 感謝する, 礼を言う **thank ～ for** ～に対して礼を言う 名《-s》感謝, 謝意

□ **that** 形 その, あの 代 ①それ, あれ, その [あの] 人 [物] ②《関係代名詞》～である… 接 ～ということ, ～なので, ～だから 副 そんなに, それほど

□ **the** 冠 ①その, あの ②《形容詞の前で》～な人々 **on the right** 右 [右側] に **sit in the corner** 〔部屋の〕隅に座る 副《– ＋比較級, – ＋比較級》～すればするほど…

□ **their** 代 彼 (女) らの, それらの

□ **them** 代 彼 (女) らを [に], それらを [に]

□ **then** 副 その時 (に・は), それから, 次に 名 その時 形 その当時の

□ **there** 副 ①そこに [で・の], そこへ, あそこへ ②《– is [are] ～》～がある [いる] **over there** あそこに 名 そこ

□ **these** 代 これら, これ 形 これらの, この

□ **they** 代 ①彼 (女) らは [が], それらは [が] ② (一般の) 人々は [が]

□ **thing** 名 ①物, 事 ②《-s》事情, 事柄 ③《one's -s》持ち物, 身の回り品 ④人, やつ

□ **think** 動 思う, 考える

□ **third** 名 第3 (の人 [物]) 形 第3の, 3番の

□ **this** 形 ①この, こちらの, これを ②今の, 現在の 代 ①これ, この人

[物] ②今, ここ

□ **though** 接 ①～にもかかわらず, ～だが ②たとえ～でも **even though** ～であるけれども, ～にもかかわらず 副 しかし

□ **thought** 動 think (思う) の過去, 過去分詞 名 考え, 意見

□ **three** 名 3 (の数字), 3人 [個] 形 3の, 3人 [個] の

□ **through** 前 ～を通して, ～中を [に], ～中 副 ①通して ②終わりまで, まったく, すっかり **run through** 走り抜ける

□ **tie** 動 結ぶ, 束縛する

□ **time** 名 ①時, 時間, 歳月 ②時期 ③期間 ④時代 ⑤回, 倍 **any time** いつでも **at any time of day or night** 昼夜を問わずいつでも **every time** ～するときはいつも **next time** 次回は 動 時刻を決める, 時間を計る

□ **tired** 動 tire (疲れる) の過去, 過去分詞 形 ①疲れた, くたびれた ②あきた, うんざりした

□ **to** 前 ①《方向・変化》～へ, ～に, ～の方へ ②《程度・時間》～まで ③《適合・付加・所属》～に ④《－＋動詞の原形》～するために [の], ～する, ～すること **be close to** ～に近い **decide to do** ～することに決める **go to bed** 床につく, 寝る **jump to one's feet** 飛び起きる **need to do** ～する必要がある **next to** ～のとなりに, ～の次に **ready to** いつでも～できる, ～する心構えができている **say to oneself** ひとり言を言う, 心に思う **start to do** ～し始める **stop to** ～しようと立ち止まる **tell ～ to …** ～に…するように言う **wake up to** ～で目を覚ます

□ **together** 副 ①一緒に, ともに ②同時に

□ **told** 動 tell (話す) の過去, 過去分詞

□ **too** 副 ①～も (また) ②あまりに～すぎる, とても～

□ **took** 動 take (取る) の過去

□ **top** 名 ①頂上, 首位 ②こま **on top of** ～の上 (部) に 形 いちばん上の

□ **tortoise** 名 カメ (亀)

□ **town** 名 町, 都会, 都市

□ **tree** 名 ①木, 樹木, 木製のもの ②系図

□ **tried** 動 try (試みる) の過去, 過去分詞 形 試験済みの, 信頼できる

□ **try** 動 ①やってみる, 試みる ②努力する, 努める

□ **two** 名 2 (の数字), 2人 [個] 形 2の, 2人 [個] の **In a day or two** 一両日中に

U

□ **under** 前 ①《位置》～の下 [に] ②《状態》～で, ～を受けて, ～のもと ③《数量》～以下 [未満] の, ～より下の 形 下の, 下部の 副 下に [で], 従属 [服従] して

□ **up** 副 ①上へ, 上がって, 北へ ②立って, 近づいて ③向上して, 増して **catch up with** ～に追いつく **come up** 近づいてくる, 浮上する,

水面へ上ってくる **jump up** 素早く立ち上がる **look up** 見上げる **pick up** 拾い上げる **run up** ～に走り寄る **stand up** 立ち上がる **wake up** 起きる，目を覚ます **wake up to** ～で目を覚ます 前 ①～の上(の方)へ，高い方へ ②(道)に沿って 形 上向きの，上りの

□ **us** 代 私たちを[に] **let us** どうか私たちに～させてください

□ **use** 動 ①使う，用いる ②費やす 名 使用，用途

V

□ **very** 副 とても，非常に，まったく **very well** 結構，よろしい 形 本当の，きわめて，まさしくその

□ **visit** 動 訪問する 名 訪問

□ **voice** 名 ①声，音声 ②意見，発言権 動 声に出す，言い表す

W

□ **wait** 動 ①待つ，《－ for ～》～を待つ ②延ばす，延ばせる，遅らせる ③《－ on [upon] ～》～に仕える，給仕をする

□ **wake** 動 ①目が覚める，起きる，起こす ②奮起する **wake up** 起きる，目を覚ます **wake up to** ～で目を覚ます

□ **walk** 動 歩く，歩かせる，散歩する **walk along** (前へ)歩く，～に沿って歩く **walk around** 歩き回る，ぶらぶら歩く **walk away** 立ち去る，遠ざかる 名 歩くこと，散歩

□ **wall** 名 ①壁，塀 ②障壁 動 壁[塀]で囲む，ふさぐ

□ **want** 動 ほしい，望む，～したい，～してほしい 名 欠乏，不足

□ **warm** 形 ①暖かい，温暖な ②思いやりのある，愛情のある 動 暖まる，暖める

□ **warn** 動 警告する，用心させる

□ **was** 動《beの第1・第3人称単数現在am, isの過去》～であった，(～に)いた[あった]

□ **wash** 動 ①洗う，洗濯する ②押し流す[される] 名 洗うこと

□ **watch** 動 ①じっと見る，見物する ②注意[用心]する，監視する 名 ①警戒，見張り ②腕時計

□ **wave** 名 ①波 ②(手などを)振ること 動 ①揺れる，揺らす，波立つ ②(手などを振って)合図する

□ **we** 代 私たちは[が]

□ **wear** 動 ①着る，着ている，身につける ②疲れる，消耗する，すり切れる 名 ①着用 ②衣類

□ **week** 名 週，1週間

□ **well** 副 ①うまく，上手に ②十分に，よく，かなり **very well** 結構，よろしい 間 へえ，まあ，ええと

□ **went** 動 go (行く)の過去

□ **were** 動《beの2人称単数・複数の過去》～であった，(～に)いた[あった]

□ **what** 代 ①何が[を・に] ②《関係代名詞》～するところのもの[こと] 形 ①何の，どんな ②なんと ③～するだけの 副 いかに，どれほ

A B C D E F G H I J K L M N O P Q R S T U V W X Y Z

ど

□ **when** 副 ①いつ ②《関係副詞》～するところの, ～するとその時, ～するとき 接 ～の時, ～するとき 代 いつ

□ **where** 副 ①どこに[で] ②《関係副詞》～するところの, そしてそこで, ～するところ 接 ～なところに[へ], ～するところに[へ] 代 ①どこ, どの点 ②～するところの

□ **while** 接 ①～の間(に), ～する間(に) ②一方, ～なのに 名 しばらくの間, 一定の時 **for a while** しばらく(の間), 少しの間

□ **who** 代 ①誰が[は], どの人 ②《関係代名詞》～するところの(人)

□ **why** 副 ①なぜ, どうして ②《関係副詞》～するところの(理由) 間 ①おや, まあ ②もちろん, なんだって ③ええと

□ **wife** 名 妻, 夫人

□ **will** 助 ～だろう, ～しよう, する(つもりだ)

□ **win** 動 勝つ, 獲得する, 達する 名 勝利, 成功

□ **winter** 名 冬

□ **wise** 形 賢明な, 聡明な, 博学の

□ **with** 前 ①《同伴・付随・所属》～と一緒に, ～を身につけて, ～とともに ②《様態》～(の状態)で, ～して ③《手段・道具》～で, ～を使って **agree with** (人)に同意する **catch up with** ～に追いつく

□ **woke** 動 wake (目が覚める)の過去

□ **wolf** 名 オオカミ(狼)

□ **wolves** 名 wolf (オオカミ)の複数

□ **won** 動 win (勝つ)の過去, 過去分詞

□ **wood** 名 ①《しばしば-s》森, 林 ②木材, まき

□ **work** 動 ①働く, 勉強する, 取り組む ②機能[作用]する, うまくいく 名 ①仕事, 勉強 ②職 ③作品

□ **would** 助《will の過去》①～するだろう, ～するつもりだ ②～したものだ

□ **write** 動〔文字や言葉などを〕書く

□ **wrote** 動 write (書く)の過去

Y

□ **year** 名 ①年, 1年 ②学年, 年度 ③～歳 **for ~ years** ～年間, ～年にわたって

□ **yes** 副 はい, そうです

□ **you** 代 ①あなた(方)は[が], あなた(方)を[に] ②(一般に)人は **How can you** どうして～できるのか

□ **young** 形 若い, 幼い, 青年の

ステップラダー・シリーズ
イソップ物語

2020年11月6日　第1刷発行
2024年 4月6日　第2刷発行

原著者　イソップ

発行者　浦　晋亮

発行所　IBCパブリッシング株式会社
〒162-0804 東京都新宿区中里町29番3号 菱秀神楽坂ビル
Tel. 03-3513-4511　Fax. 03-3513-4512
www.ibcpub.co.jp

印　刷　株式会社シナノパブリッシングプレス
装　幀　久保頼三郎
イラスト　ながたかず
リライト　ニーナ・ウェグナー
ナレーション　ケイティ・アドラー
録音スタジオ　株式会社巧芸創作

ISBN978-4-7946-0642-6